Early Talk

Rhymes, Movement, And Simple Songs To Familiar Tunes

by Connie Smrke

Incentive Publications, Inc.
Nashville, Tennessee

Cover and illustrations by Dianna Richey
Edited by Sherri Y. Lewis

ISBN 0-86530-208-1

© Copyright 1991 by Incentive Publications, Inc., Nashville, TN. All rights reserved. No part of this publication may be reproduced, stored in a retrieval system, or transmitted in any form or by any means (electronic, mechanical, photocopying, recording, or otherwise) without prior written permission from Incentive Publications, Inc., with the exception below.

Permission is hereby granted to the purchaser of one copy of EARLY TALK to reproduce, in sufficient quantities for meeting yearly classroom needs.

Table Of Contents

Introduction..8

September

Good-bye Summer, Hello Fall (Seasons) 11
No More (Seasons) 12
School Days (Seasons) 13
It's School Time (Seasons) 14
School Bells (Counting, Time) 15
School (Manners & Health) 16
Counting (Counting 1 - 10) 17
Ten Little Children (Counting 1 - 10) 18
Five Little Children (Counting 1 - 5, Subtraction) 19
Ten Little Children (Counting 1 - 10, Subtraction) 20
Skipping Song (Counting 1 - 5, Movement) 22
Little Children (Social Awareness) 23
Little Child (Self-Awareness) 24
Autumn Leaves (Seasons) 25
Open The Door (Seasons) 26

October

Getting Ready For Halloween (Seasons)..29
What A Fright (Seasons)...30
Halloween Night (Seasons) 31
Halloween (Seasons)..32
Tricks Or Treats (Seasons) 33
A Little Witch (Seasons)..34
A Magic Brew (Short "A") 35
Costumes (Seasons) 36
Witches (Counting 1 - 5, Addition) 37
Strange Things (Counting 1 - 5, Subtraction)...38
Halloween Safety (Safety) 40

November

November (Seasons)...43
Thanksgiving Day (Social Studies, Seasons) 44
Thank-You (Social Awareness)...45
The Pilgrim's March (Social Studies) 46
I'm A Little Pilgrim (Self-Awareness, Movement)..47

Turkeys (Seasons)..48
Six Little Turkeys (Counting, Seasons).....................................49
Thanksgiving Things (Seasons)...50
Little Turkeys (Movement)..52
Turkey Talk (Positional Concepts)..53
Counting Rhymes (Counting 1 - 10)..54

December
Santa Is Coming (Seasons)..59
Christmas Is Coming (Seasons)...60
Ten Little Elves (Counting) 61
Eight Reindeer (Seasons)...62

January
Surprise (Seasons) 65
Snowflakes, Snowflakes (Seasons)..66
Snowflakes Falling (Seasons)...67
Snow (Seasons)..68
Poor Mr. Snowman (Social Awareness)....................................69
Snowman (Seasons)...70
Funny Little Snowman (Social Awareness) 71
S Is For Snowman (Consonant Sound "S")...............................72
S-S-S-S-S (Positional Concepts)..73
Riddles (Problem-Solving, Listening)..74

February
February (Seasons)...77
Mr. Groundhog (Seasons) 78
Penguins (Seasons)..79
Polar Bear (Science) 80
Up In The Arctic (Science)...81
Igloo (Social Studies)..82
February 14th (Seasons, Social Awareness) 83
Will You Be My Valentine? (Seasons, Social Awareness)..........84

March
March (Seasons)...87
The Month Of March (Seasons)..88

I Love Green (Color Green) 89
Look Out! (Seasons) 90
Look At The Leprechaun (Seasons) 91
Counting Leprechauns (Counting By Twos) 92
Five Little Leprechauns (Counting 1 - 5, Subtraction) 93
Naughty Little Fellows (Counting 1 - 5, Subtraction) 94
I'm A Little Leprechaun (Seasons) 96

April

Spring In The Playground (Seasons) 99
Spring Is Here (Seasons) 100
Wake Up (Seasons) 102
New Life (Seasons) 103
Sights Of Spring (Seasons) 104
Something In The Air (Seasons) 105
Birds (Seasons) 106
Counting In Spring (Counting 1 - 10) 107
Animals Returning (Seasons) 108
Rain (Science/Weather) 110

May

May (Seasons) 113
Flowers (Counting, Addition, Movement) 114
Follow The Leader (Animals And Their Young, Movement) 116
Sights In May (Positional Concepts) 118

June

June (Seasons) 121
Little Children (Seasons) 122
Field Trip (Numbers, Addition) 123
Counting, Playing Games (Counting 1 - 10, Self-Awareness) 124
Be Like…(Positional Concepts) 126

Introduction

EARLY TALK is a fun, participatory collection of rhyming and action verses and singing verses written to the tune of favorite children's songs, such as "I'm A Little Teapot" and "This Old Man."

Easily adaptable to levels preK-2, EARLY TALK provides a creative way for children to learn social awareness skills, numbers and counting, increase vocabulary, and develop language skills and verbal communication skills.

Since most children enjoy learning in a play situation, they should respond more readily to a rhyme rather than a command. Arranged by month for the teacher's convenience, these rhyming activities will encourage children to use lots of movement and imagination.

The table of contents provides an easy reference to the skill emphasis of each activity. Stated skills at the bottom of each page allow you to choose immediately which skill to emphasize!

Rhyming verses intended for adaptation to children's songs are indicated under the title as are those intended for action verses.

EARLY TALK should provide hours of learning fun through song and action!

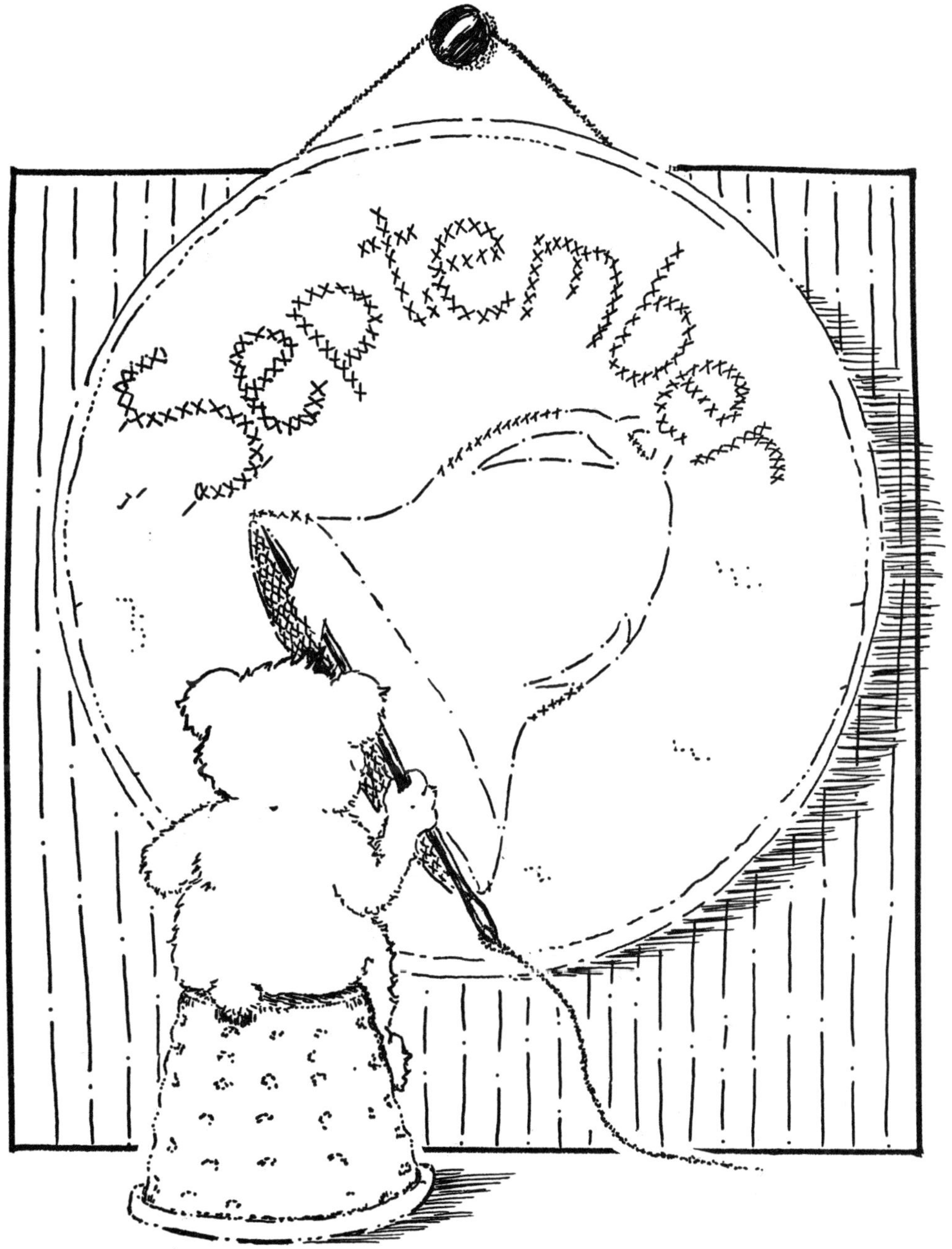
September

Good-bye Summer, Hello Fall

(Tune - "Twinkle Twinkle Little Star")

Good-bye summer,
Hello fall.
Summer's memories we'll recall.
School bells ringing,
Soon we'll hear,
Children coming from far and near.
Good-bye summer,
Hello fall.
Time has come to heed the call.

Seasons

No More

No more swimming,
No more sun,
No more fishing; the time has come
To find our books and
Find our class.
September has come so fast.

No more picnics
Or sleeping in.
No more baseball games to win.
School days now
Are here to stay.
The month of June seems far away.

School Days

The alarm clock rings,
You open your eyes.
The day begins,
You have to rise.

Brush your teeth,
Comb your hair.
Brand new things
For you to wear.

Look both ways
As you cross the street.
Get on the bus
And find a seat.

Today is the day
That school begins.
You can hardly wait
To meet your friends.

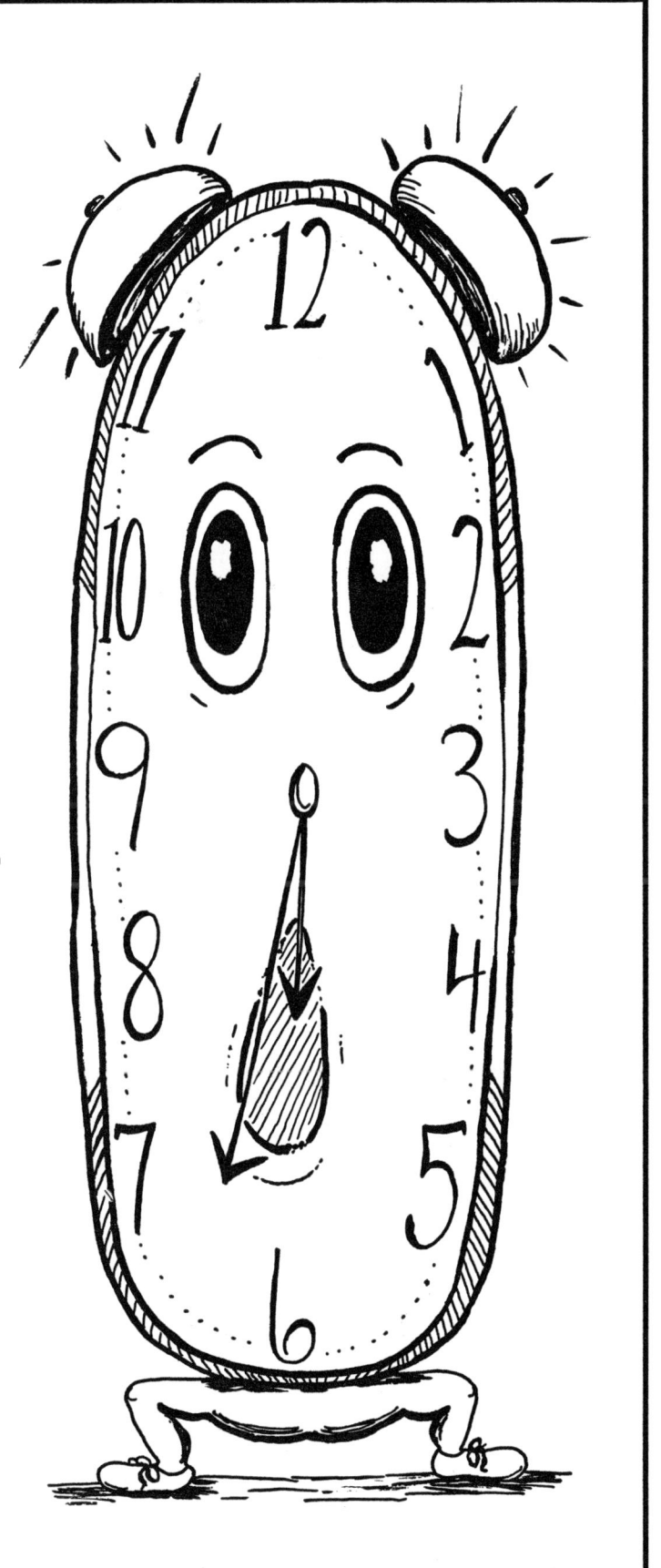

Seasons

It's School Time

Buy a new school bag,
Buy new clothes,
Buy new shoes –
I can't wear those!
Making lunches,
Making a friend,
Making projects –
It's school time again!

School Bells

The bell rings and I count to ten.
Cutting and pasting and numbers again.

The bell rings and it's time to play.
Skipping and marbles and tag today.

The bell rings and in we go.
Why does the time go so slow?

The bell rings and it's time to eat.
Sandwiches, juice, a special treat.

The bell rings and we leave once more.
So much to do – we're never bored!

Counting, Time

School

Sharpen your pencils,
Cover your books.
Sit up tall,
No nasty looks.

No staying up late,
You need your rest
To do your work,
To do your best.

Yes, school has started,
And work has begun.
Reading and writing,
And we'll have fun.

Manners & Health

Counting

1 2 3 4 5

Busy bees buzzing in a hive.

6 7 8 9 10

Baby birds follow mother wren.

10 9 8 7 6

Yellow-feathered friendly chicks.

5 4 3 2 1

Counting can be lots of fun.

Counting 1 - 10

Ten Little Children

(Tune - "Ten Little Indians")

One little
Two little
Three little children.

Four little
Five little
Six little children.

Seven little
Eight little
Nine little children.
Ten little children playing.

Playing in the sand and playing in the water.
Playing in the house being moms and daughters.
Cooking and cleaning, being fathers.
Ten little children playing.

Counting 1 - 10

Five Little Children

5 little children starting out for school,
One decided to break the rules.

Now there are

4 little children starting out for school,
One decided to swim in the pool.

Now there are

3 little children starting out for school,
One decided to play it cool.

Now there are

2 little children starting out for school,
One decided to ride a mule.

Now there is

1 little child starting out for school,
and he decided to search for jewels.

Now there are
Five little children sad and blue,
With homework and detentions
For a month or two.

Counting 1 - 5, Subtraction

Ten Little Children

10 Little children feeling just fine,
One got sick, and then there were **9**.

9 Little children swinging on a gate,
One stayed behind, and then there were **8**.

8 Little children, one called Kevin,
He got lost, and then there were **7**.

7 Little children gathering sticks,
One fell down, and then there were **6**.

6 Little children learning to dive,
One did a belly flop, and then there were **5**.

Counting 1 - 10, Subtraction

5 Little children hiding behind a door,
One bumped his head, and then there were **4**.

4 Little children happy as can be,
One ran away, and then there were **3**.

3 Little children dressed in blue,
One got dirty, and then there were **2**.

2 Little children playing in the sun,
One got dizzy, and then there was **1**.

1 Little child playing all alone,
She skipped away and went back home.

Skipping Song

Skipping, skipping 1, 2, 3,
Come and skip along with me.
Skipping, skipping on the floor.
Skipping, skipping count to 4.
Skipping, skipping come alive.
Skipping, skipping count to 5.

5 4 3 2 1

Skipping can be lots of fun.

Little Children

(Tune - "This Old Man")

Little children out to play
Play in water and sand all day.
With shovels, pails, and sifters, too,
There are lots of things to do.

Little children out to play
Cut and paste and model clay.
With crayons, scissors, and sticky glue,
There are lots of things to do.

Little children in grade one
They count numbers and have fun.
With sticks and numbers, fingers, too,
There are lots of things to do.

Little children in grade two
Read and write new stories for you.
With papers, pencils, computers, too,
There are lots of things to do.

Little children in grade three
Science, math, and history.
With maps and globes and charting, too,
There are lots of things to do.

Social Awareness

Little Child

(Tune - "I'm A Little Teapot")

I'm a little child.
I like to play.
I find it hard to stay in school all day.
I play in the water,
And the sand.
And I play in the marching band.

I'm a little child.
I like to play.
I learned the color red today.
Cutting and pasting,
Matching, too.
Circles and squares, old and new.

Self-Awareness

Autumn Leaves

(Tune - "London Bridge")

Autumn leaves are falling down,
Falling down,
Falling down.
Autumn leaves are falling down.
Yellow, red, orange, and brown.

September winds begin to blow,
Begin to blow,
Begin to blow.
September winds begin to blow.
We don't care cause in we go.

Seasons

Open The Door

The school bell rings,
You open the door.
Another school year
Begins once more.

Seasons

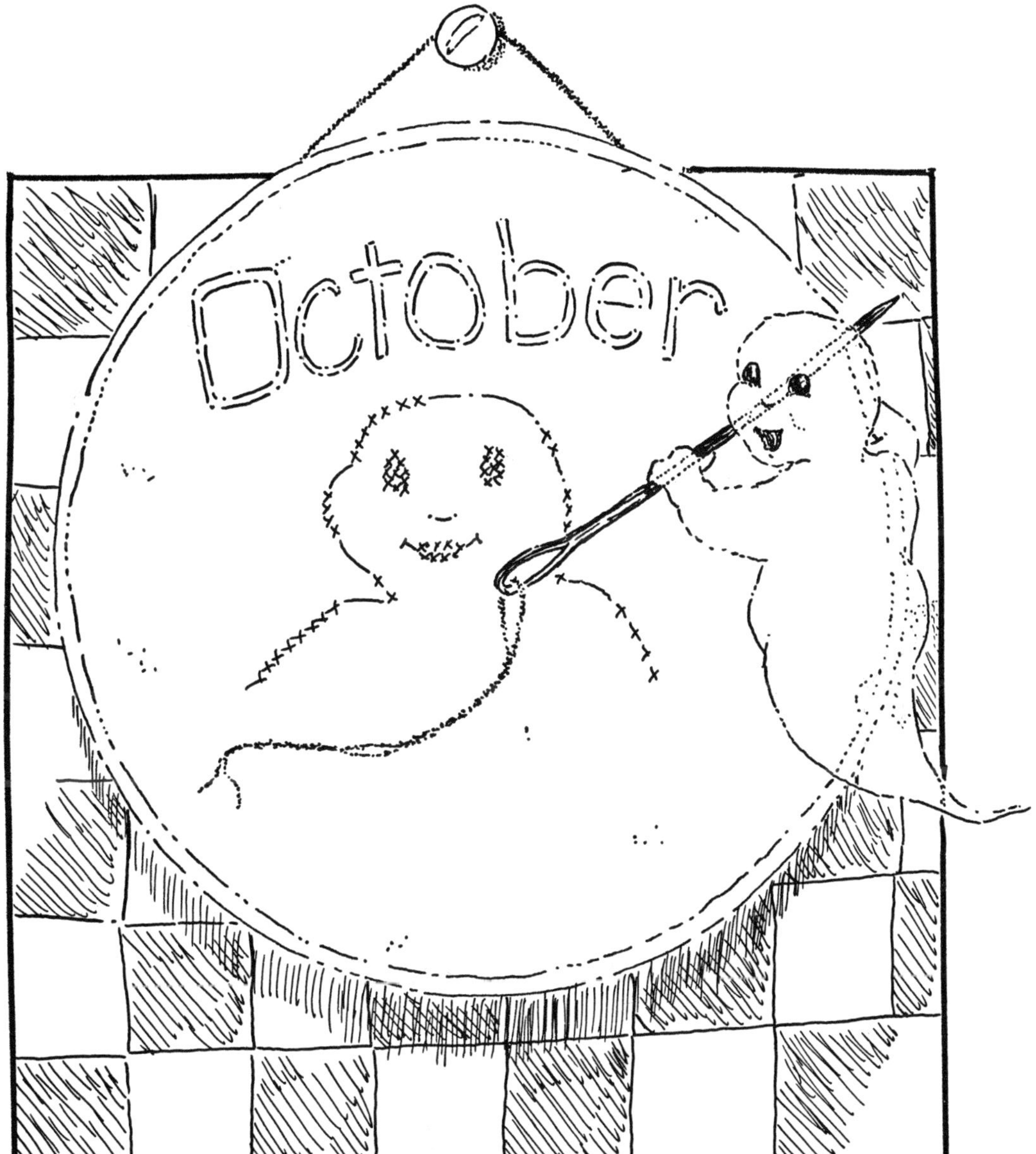
October

Getting Ready For Halloween

(Tune - "Farmer In The Dell")

The witches stir their brew.
The witches stir their brew.
They throw in all their magic things,
The witches stir their brew.

The witches find their cats.
The witches find their cats.
They put them out upon the fence,
The witches find their cats.

The witches get their brooms.
The witches get their brooms.
They dust them off and "start" them up,
The witches get their brooms.

The witches now all leave.
The witches now all leave.
They're just in time; it's Halloween,
The witches now all leave.

Seasons

What A Fright

Ghosts and goblins are everywhere.
Witches and bats fly through the air.
Werewolves, skeletons,
What a fright!
So beware cause
It's Halloween night!

BOO

Seasons

Halloween Night

(Tune - "Up On The Housetop")

Out on a dark night
You can see
Witches and bats hanging in a tree.
Skeletons and monsters are all around;
Pumpkins and goblins are on the ground.
Oh, oh, oh, watch them go,
Oh, oh, oh, now don't you know?
Halloween is finally here,
But you have nothing to fear.

Seasons

Halloween

(Tune - "Frere Jaques")

Halloween
Halloween
Will soon be here
Soon be here.
With witches and bats
Goblins and cats
It's getting near
It's getting near.

Seasons

Tricks Or Treats

(Tune - "London Bridge")

Witches riding on their brooms
　　　　　　on their brooms
　　　　　　on their brooms
Witches riding on their brooms
Flying right up to the moon.

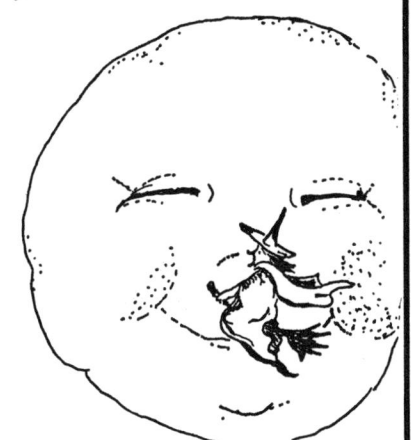

Skeletons clanking down the street
　　　　　　down the street
　　　　　　down the street
Skeletons clanking down the street
Monsters, goblins they do meet.

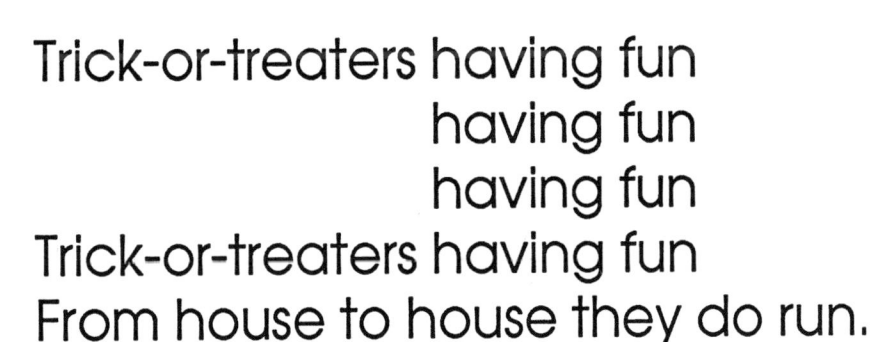

Trick-or-treaters having fun
　　　　　having fun
　　　　　having fun
Trick-or-treaters having fun
From house to house they do run.

Seasons

A Little Witch

A little old witch
Got on her broom,
Said some magic words and pointed at the moon.
But the broom only shook, and it didn't go far.
So that Halloween she had to use the car!

A Magic Brew

Stirring up a magic brew
Abracadabra - Alakazoo.
Throw in a lizard,
Throw in a bat,
But beware of the witch's cat.
Abracadabra - Alakazoo,
Stirring up a magic brew.

Short "A"

Costumes

Fairies
Princesses
Scarecrows
Bats,
This is a night for all of that!

Hobos
Turtle wars
Frogs in green,
All come out for Halloween.

Monsters
Vampires
Grizzly bears, too,

Dragons
Dinosaurs
A scary crew,
Yes, Halloween is a time for fun,
So come on out, everyone!

Witches

1 little witch was stirring her brew.
She threw in some magic,
And then there were two.

2 little witches filled with glee.
They snapped their fingers,
And then there were three.

3 little witches by the door.
They turned around,
And then there were four.

4 little witches hiding in a hive.
They all flew out,
And then there were five.

5 little witches on the run.
They all went out
To have some Halloween fun.

Counting 1 - 5, Addition

Strange Things

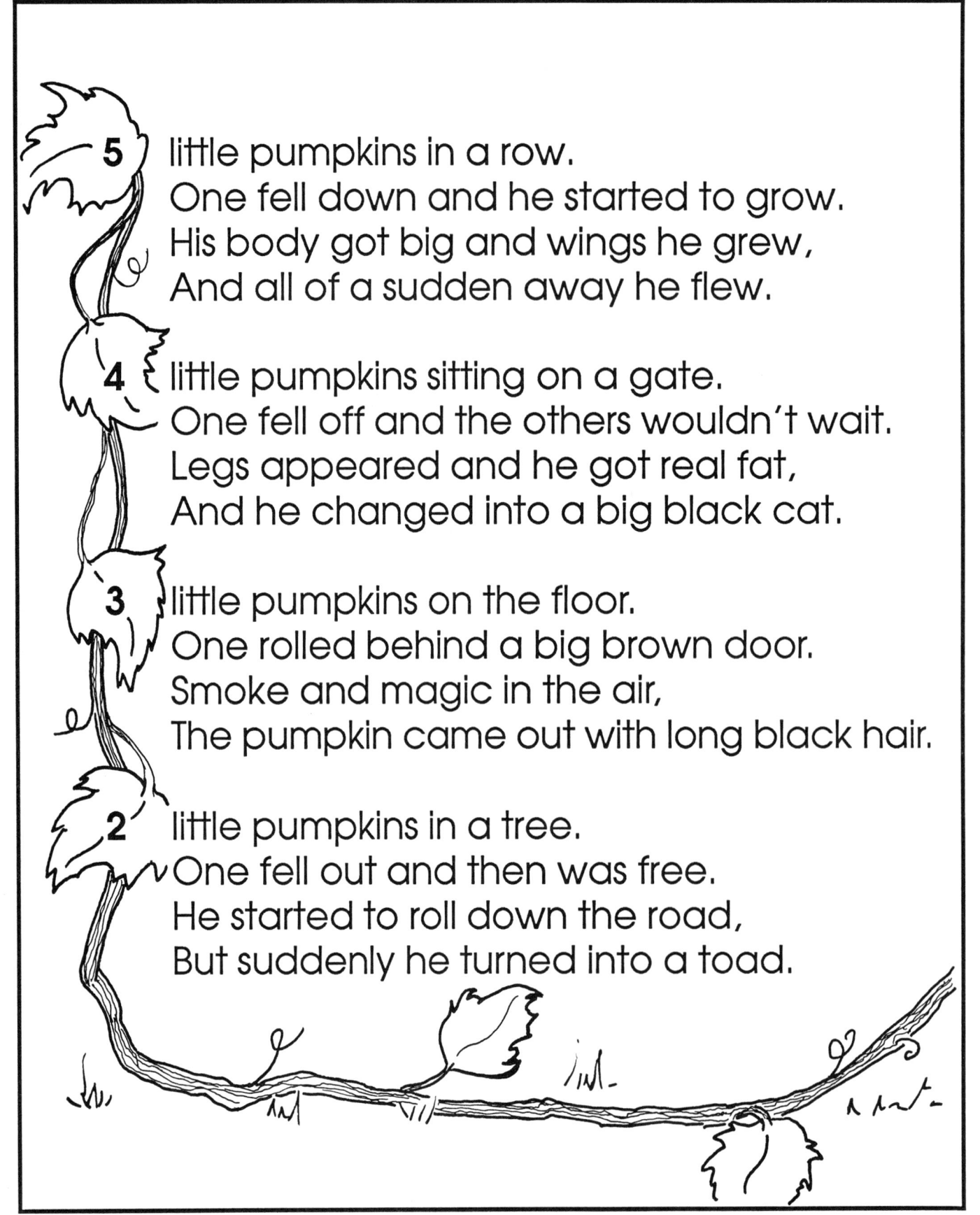

5 little pumpkins in a row.
One fell down and he started to grow.
His body got big and wings he grew,
And all of a sudden away he flew.

4 little pumpkins sitting on a gate.
One fell off and the others wouldn't wait.
Legs appeared and he got real fat,
And he changed into a big black cat.

3 little pumpkins on the floor.
One rolled behind a big brown door.
Smoke and magic in the air,
The pumpkin came out with long black hair.

2 little pumpkins in a tree.
One fell out and then was free.
He started to roll down the road,
But suddenly he turned into a toad.

Counting 1 - 5, Subtraction

1 little pumpkin all alone
Decided it was time to go back home.
But the wind blew and it got real hot,
And he turned into a witch's pot.

Now strange things are happening
But do not fear,
It's only because it's Halloween cheer.

Halloween Safety

(Tune - "I'm A Little Teapot")

I'm a trick-or-treater
Set to go.
I have a flashlight
We'll walk slow.
I always say, "Thank-you," for my treats,
And I never run across the street.

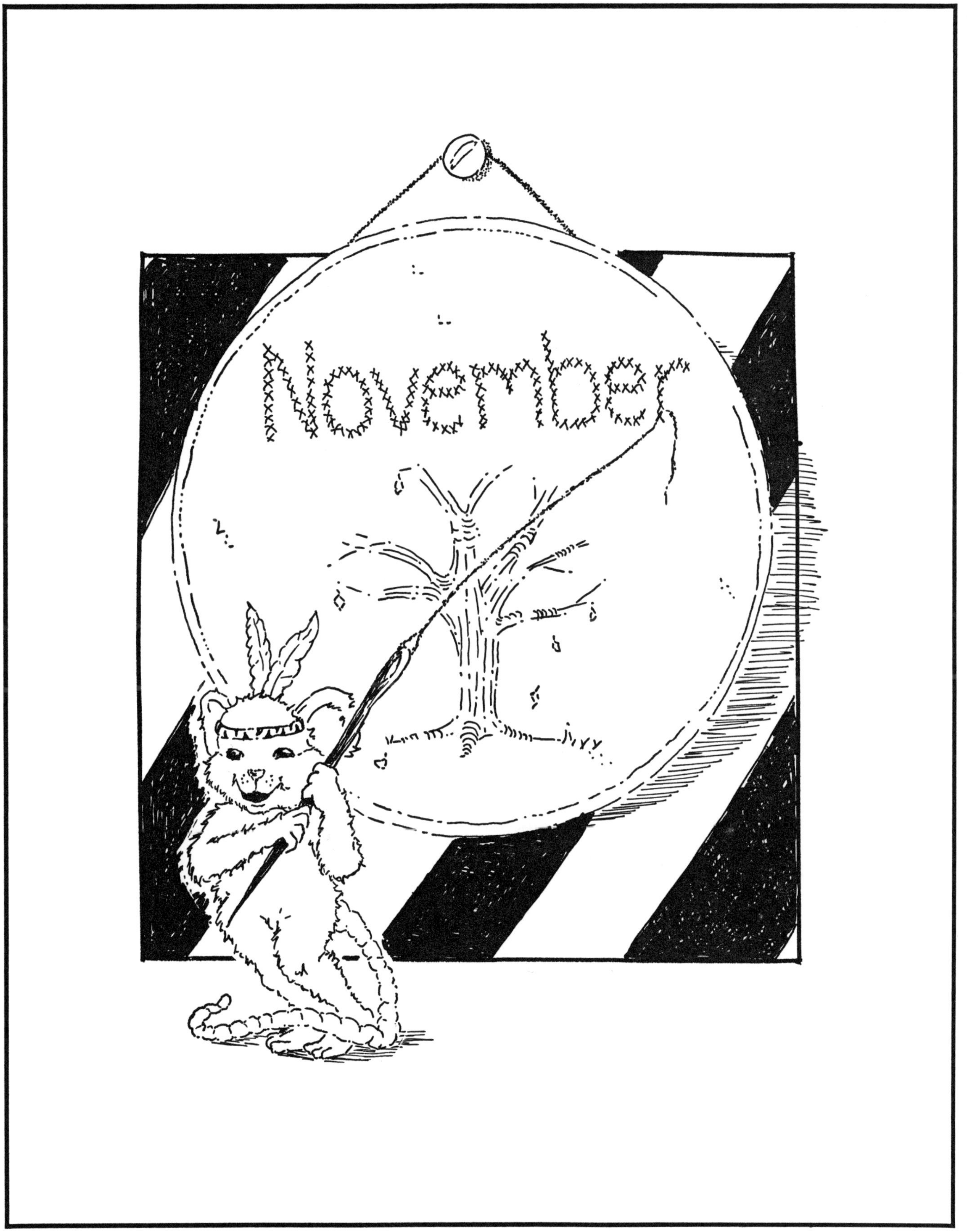
November

November

November is a month that is gloomy and gray.
Leaves are on the ground, and birds have gone away.
Children are bundled, just waiting for snow.
There's a chill in the air wherever you go.
There are times in November you some times say,
"Summer seems such a long time away."

Seasons

Thanksgiving Day

In 1620 long ago,
On the oceans the winds did blow.
It brought the ship and people, too,
To a land that was brand new.
From England's shore to Plymouth Rock,
These hearty people brought their stock.
The Indians came and lent a hand
And showed them how to farm the land,
And how to hunt, fish, and get plants to grow
And showed them other things they didn't know.
So here the pilgrims made their home
And with their friends were not alone.
They had a feast and planned to stay
And called it their Thanksgiving Day.

Social Studies, Seasons

Thank-You

(Tune - "Twinkle Twinkle Little Star")

Mother
Father
Sister, too
For these things, I'm thanking you
For my friends and my brother, too,
For these things, I thank you.

Social Awareness

The Pilgrims March

(Tune - "She'll Be Coming Around The Mountain")

Pilgrims coming over by boat from England's shores.
Pilgrims coming over by boat from England's shores.
They are coming to a new place
To worship in their own way.
Pilgrims coming over by boat from England's shores.

Social Studies

I'm A Little Pilgrim

(Tune - "I'm A Little Teapot" Action Verse)

I'm a little pilgrim
See me grow.
I can stretch and bend down low.
I can jump and turn around.
And even touch the ground.
Oh, I'm a pilgrim
See me grow.

Self-Awareness, Movement

Turkeys

Turkeys in the barnyard.
Turkeys in the hay.
Turkeys running all around
On Thanksgiving Day.

The farmer tries to catch one –
The fattest is the "winner."
And sure enough, he ends up
As Thanksgiving dinner.

Seasons

Six Little Turkeys

(Tune - "Six Little Ducks")

Six little turkeys that I once knew
Fat ones, skinny ones
There were two.
But the one little turkey with the
Funny red wattle.
He led the others with his
Gobble, gobble, gobble.
He led the others with his
Gobble, gobble, gobble.

Over the rocks and through the trees,
Turkeys wobbling in the breeze.
But the one little turkey with the
Funny red wattle.
He led the others with his
Gobble, gobble, gobble.

Counting, Seasons

Thanksgiving Things

(Tune - "Farmer In The Dell")

The turkeys in the pen,
The turkeys in the pen.
All the children come and see,
The turkeys in the pen.

The pilgrims on the boat,
The pilgrims on the boat.
All the children come and see,
The pilgrims on the boat.

The Indians in the field,
The Indians in the field.
All the children come and see,
The Indians in the field.

Seasons

The pumpkins in the patch,
The pumpkins in the patch.
All the children come and see,
The pumpkins in the patch.

The corn on the cob,
The corn on the cob.
All the children come and see,
The corn on the cob.

The butter in the churn,
The butter in the churn.
All the children come and see,
The butter in the churn.

Little Turkeys

(Tune - "This Old Man")

Little turkeys walking by.
They can move from side-to-side
With a wobble here and a wobble there,
They can wobble everywhere.

Little turkeys making sounds.
They can talk as they move around
With a gobble here and a gobble there,
They can gobble everywhere.

Movement

Turkey Talk

(Tune - "Row, Row, Row Your Boat")

Gobble, gobble turkey talk,
Turkeys all around.
Standing up and sitting down,
Turkeys on the ground.

Counting Rhymes

1 2 3 4 5

All the turkeys come alive.

5 4 3 2 1

Turkeys having lots of fun.

6 7 8 9 10

Turkeys running round again.

10 9 8 7 6

Turkeys, turkeys in a fix.

5 10 15 20,

Filling up the horn of plenty.

Carrots, cabbages, apples, too,

Things to eat for me and you.

25 30 35 more,

Now there are turkeys at the door.

40 45 50, too,

Now the turkeys are in the stew.

Counting By Fives

2 4 6 8 10

Turkeys marching in a pen.

10 8 6 4 2

Turkeys, turkeys in a stew.

Counting By Twos

December

Santa Is Coming

(Tune - "I'm A Little Teapot")

Santa is coming
On his sleigh.
From the North Pole far away.
His bag is filled with lots of toys.
For good girls and boys.
Yes, Santa is coming
On his sleigh.

Christmas Is Coming

(Tune - "Up On The Housetop")

Christmas is coming
Don't you fear.
Santa Claus and eight reindeer.
Pulling a sleigh all filled with toys.
Bringing joy to girls and boys.
Ho, ho, ho, now watch him go.
Ho, ho, ho, he's never slow.
Filling stockings, then he leaves.
All is set on Christmas Eve.

Ten Little Elves

Ten little elves working hard today
To help Santa on his way.
Fixing trucks and dolls and toys,
Making things for girls and boys.

But one little elf sat all alone,
He started to cry and he went back home.
He couldn't help that he was too small,
They said he was no use at all.

Then Santa came and saved the day
And placed him on his great big sleigh.
Now the elf shouts, "Merry Christmas," to all,
And suddenly he feels ten feet tall!

Eight Reindeer

(Tune - "Six Little Ducks")

Eight reindeer pulling Santa's sleigh
Left the North Pole one cold day
With lots of toys in a great big pack
And jolly Santa sitting on the back.

Over the rooftops, in the house
Santa is as quiet as a mouse
When he's filling stockings.
And when he's done
He shouts, "Merry Christmas to everyone!"
"Merry Christmas to everyone!"

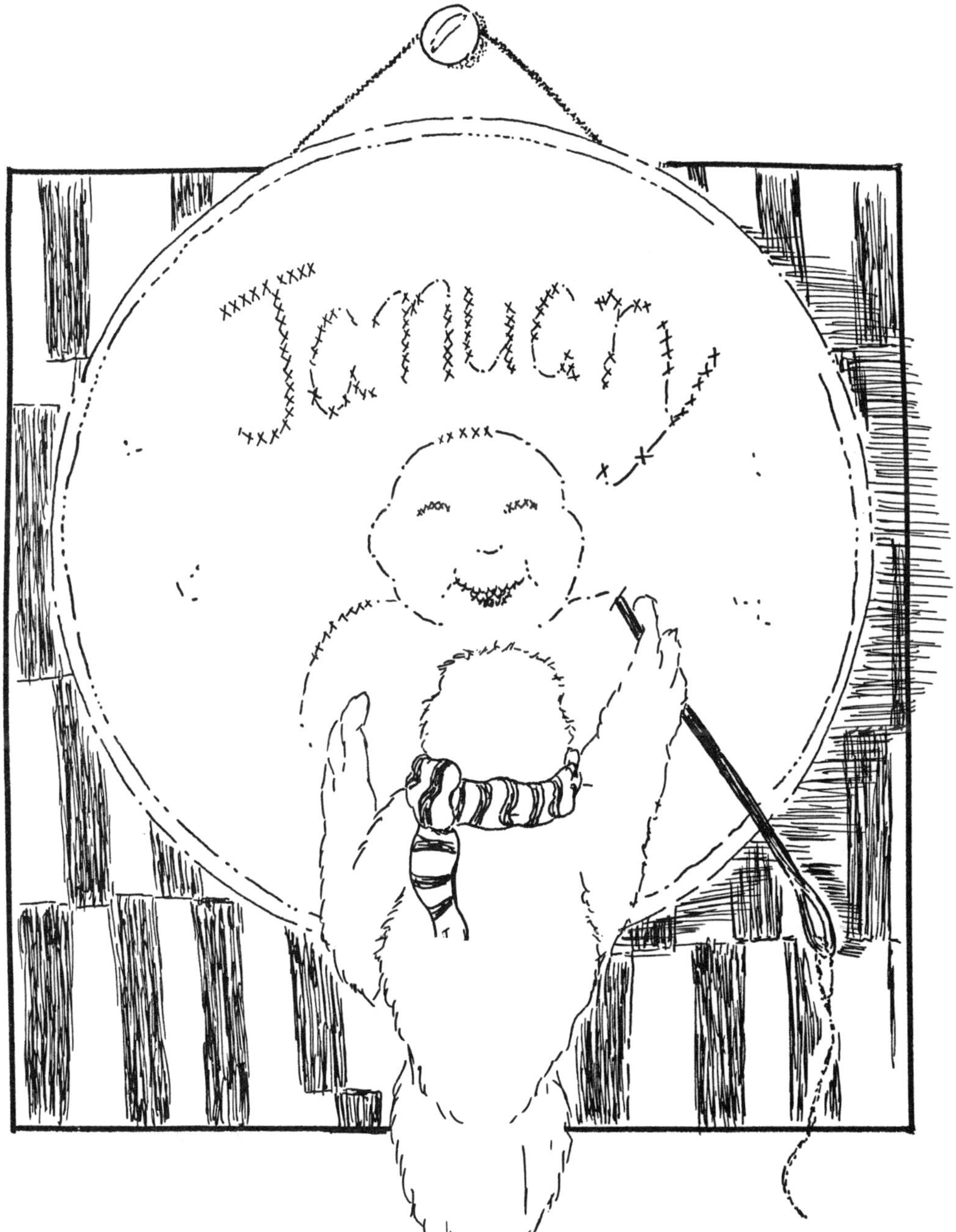
January

Surprise

I opened my eyes and my room was bright.
I wondered what happened outside last night.
I opened the windows and let everyone know
The world was covered with fluffy white snow.
I grabbed my mittens, my scarf, and my suit
And pulled on my brand new winter boots.
I ran outside and I started to play,
And hoped that the snow was here to stay.

Snowflakes, Snowflakes

(Tune - "Twinkle Twinkle Little Star")

Snowflakes falling
One by one,
Time to play and have some fun.
Build a snowman
Snowballs, too,
Come and see what you can do.
Snowflakes falling
One by one,
Time to play and have some fun.

Snowflakes Falling

(Tune - "Up On The Housetop")

Snowflakes are falling on the ground
On our houses and in our town
On my nose and in my hair
Snowflakes are falling everywhere.
Oh, oh, oh, out we go,
Oh, oh, oh, in the snow
Making snowmen
Sliding, too,
There are lots of things to do.

Seasons

Snow

(Tune - "This Old Man")

Snow is falling on the ground
We can make things all around
Like snowmen, snowballs
Snow forts, too.
There are lots of things to do.
Snow is falling come and see
You can have some fun with me
Sliding, skating, skiing, too,
There are lots of things to do.

Seasons

Poor Mr. Snowman

Poor Mr. Snowman
Dressed in white
Standing in the cold wind,
Freezing all night.
I would bring him inside
And make him feel better,
But Mommy says he likes
This chilly weather.

Social Awareness

Snowman

(Tune - "I'm A Little Teapot")

I'm a little snowman
Round and fat
I have a broomstick
I have a hat.
With my friends
I play in the snow.
But when the sun shines
It's time to go.

Seasons

Funny Little Snowman

A funny little snowman
Sat in our yard today.
He said, "Come out and play with me
Before I melt away!"
He placed a hat upon his head
And began to dance around.
We laughed and sang some silly songs
And fell upon the ground.
And when the sun began to shine
Beating down that day,
My funny little snowman
Began to melt away.

S Is For Snowman

S is for snowman
round and fat.
Sitting outside wearing a hat.
I brought him inside and
sat him on the mat,
and before very long,
the snowman was flat.

S is for snowman,
skiis, and sled.

S is for snuggling
safe in bed.

S is for scarf
socks, and sun.

S is for snowflakes
melting on my tongue.

Consonant Sound "S"

S-S-S-S-S

Seven silly snowmen
Sitting side-by-side.
Out came the sun,
And they had to hide.
Two behind the sled
Two behind the tree,
Two behind the snowbank,
And one behind me.

Positional Concepts

Riddles

I have six sides
And I fall from the sky.
I land on your nose,
I land on your eye.
Can you guess what name have I?

_____

Round balls of snow
And a funny-looking hat,
A broomstick and a carrot
And some buttons that are black.
What can you make from all of that?

_____

I travel through the snow
And you sit on me.
I make a lot of noise,
And on the bottom there are skiis.
What is the name that you call me?

_____

You can sit on me
And slide in the snow.
Or someone can pull you
Wherever you go.
What is the name that I want you to know?

_____

Problem-Solving, Listening Skills

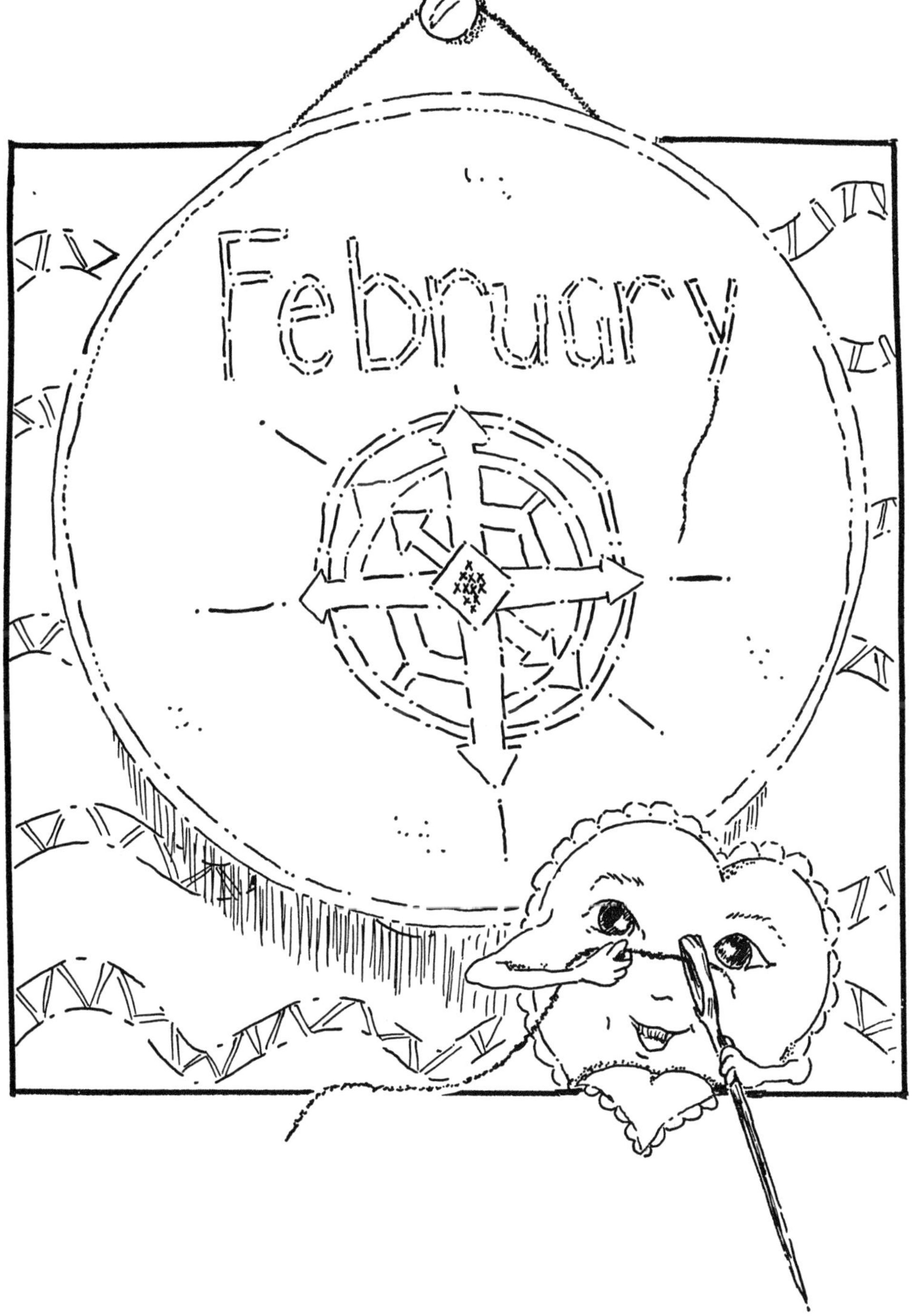
February

February

February's freezing.
Where do we go?
Animals hibernate under the snow.
People are bundled
From their heads to their feet.
Children are covered with blankets so deep.
Icicles are hanging in a row.
Frost is on the windows –
Crunchy snow.

February's freezing.
Where do we go?
Beside the fire's
Cozy, warm glow.

Mr. Groundhog

Poor Mr. Groundhog
Asleep underground.
On February 2nd he awakes
And looks around.
And if the sun is shining,
And his shadow's on the ground,
He runs back to his cozy bed,
And for six weeks can't be found.
But if the day is cloudy
And his shadow he can't see,
Winter will be over, for groundhog,
You, and me.

Seasons

Penguins

(Tune - "I'm A Little Teapot")

I am black and white.
I like the snow.
I waddle sideways.
I like the cold.
"Penguin" is the name
I'm called today.
I am black and white
I like the snow.

Seasons

Polar Bear

I am white
And big and bold.
I live in the ice and cold.
I can be dangerous
So beware,
My name is "polar bear."

Science

Up In The Arctic

Up in the arctic all around,
Polar bears and walruses
Can be found.
Eskimos, dog sleds
Igloos, blue,
Arctic fox, harp seals
Live here, too.
The arctic is covered by ice and snow,
And the weather is cold
Wherever you go.

Igloo

I am a house
Made of ice and snow.
Eskimos lived in me long ago.
Cold is where I had to be,
"Igloo" is what you call me.

Social Studies

February 14th

February 14th is a special day
To send someone a gift of love
In a special way.
You can send some candy
In a box of blue,
Or you can send a special poem
Written just by you.

Seasons, Social Awareness

Will You Be My Valentine?

(Tune - "London Bridge Is Falling Down")

Will you be my Valentine?
Valentine?
Valentine?
Will you be my Valentine?
It'll make me feel fine.

(Tune - "Frere Jacques")

Will you be my Valentine?
Valentine?
Valentine?
We'll be friends forever
In all kinds of weather.
You and I – Valentine.

Seasons, Social Awareness

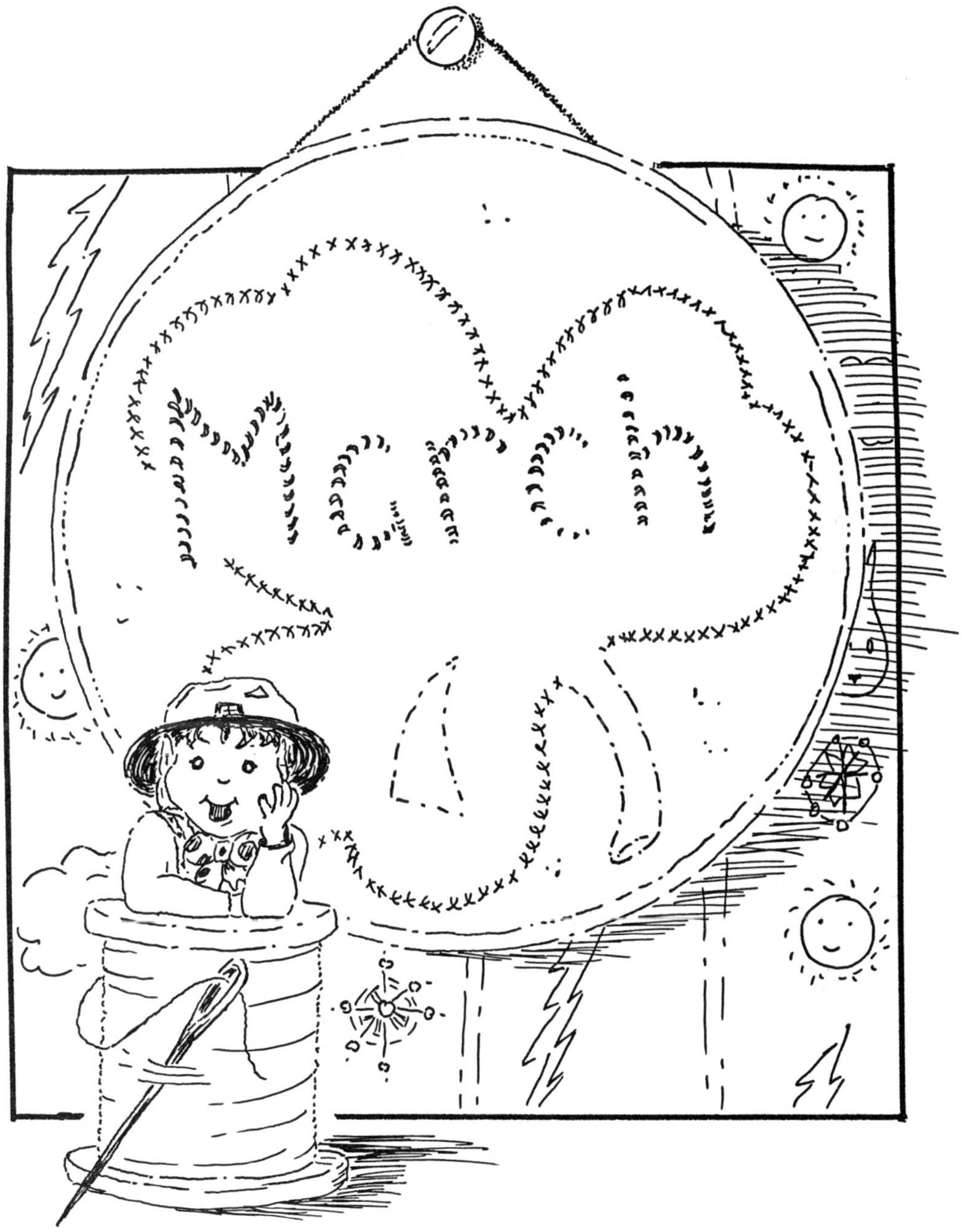
March

March

March is the month that is in-between
Christmas and toys and things that are green.
The weather can be snowy or sunny and warm,
Or we can even have a major storm.
March is the month that is in-between.

Seasons

The Month of March

March is a month that is hard to know.
Sometimes it rains and sometimes it snows.
Like a lion it roars and boldly begins,
Then like a lamb, it gently ends
April rolls in, ready to go,
But March is a month that is hard to know.

Seasons

I Love Green

(Tune - "Mary Had A Little Lamb")

I love green oh yes I do.
Yes I do.
Yes I do.
I love green oh yes I do.
Green is a frog.

(Let children continue to sing and change endings as follows.)

Green is a turtle.

Green is a tree.

Green is a shamrock.

Green is my sweater.

Green is a crayon.

Green is a lime.

Green is the grass.

Color Green

Look Out!

(Tune - "Row, Row, Row Your Boat")

Look out here they come
Little men in green.
St. Patrick's Day will soon be here
And they will soon be seen.

Happy St. Patrick's Day

(Tune - "Happy Birthday To You")

Happy St. Patrick's Day to you.
Happy St. Patrick's Day to you.
Happy St. Patrick's Day,
Happy St. Patrick's Day.
Happy St. Patrick's Day to you!

Look At The Leprechaun

(Tune - "Up On The Housetop")

Look at the leprechaun tiny and green
Hiding in places where he can't be seen.
He's full of magic, mischief, too,
Look out now he's after you!
Oh, oh, oh
Watch him go.
Oh, oh, oh
He's never slow.
A little leprechaun you can't hold,
He's always filling his pot of gold.

Seasons

Counting Leprechauns

Leprechauns counting as they play
In and out of the sun all day.

2   4   6   8   10

Leprechauns running round again.

12   14   16   18   20

Leprechauns running round a plenty.

22   24   26   28   30

Leprechauns running round in a flurry.

32   34   36   38   40

Leprechauns running round in a dory.

42   44   46   48   50

Leprechauns counting are quite nifty.

Counting By Twos

Five Little Leprechauns

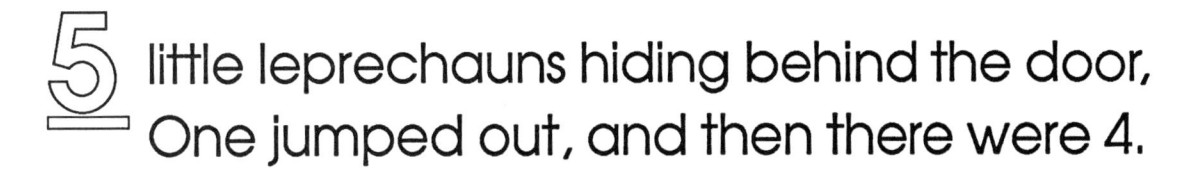

5 little leprechauns hiding behind the door,
One jumped out, and then there were 4.

4 little leprechauns hiding in a tree,
One fell out, and then there were 3.

3 little leprechauns hiding in a shoe,
One got lost, and then there were 2.

2 little leprechauns playing in the sun,
One disappeared, and then there was 1.

1 little leprechaun was very bold,
He ran away with the pot of gold!

Counting 1 - 5, Subtraction

Naughty Little Fellows

Five little leprechauns
Looking for gold.
Naughty little fellows–
Never do as they are told.

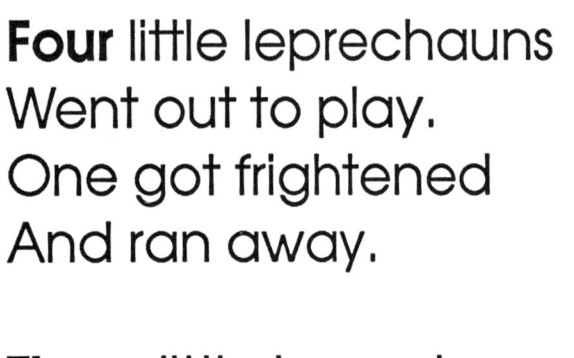

Four little leprechauns
Went out to play.
One got frightened
And ran away.

Three little leprechauns
Didn't know what to do.
One went away,
And then there were two.

Counting 1 - 5, Subtraction

Two little leprechauns
Wanted to have fun.
One stayed behind,
And then there was one.

One little leprechaun
Left all alone.
He got sick,
So he went home.

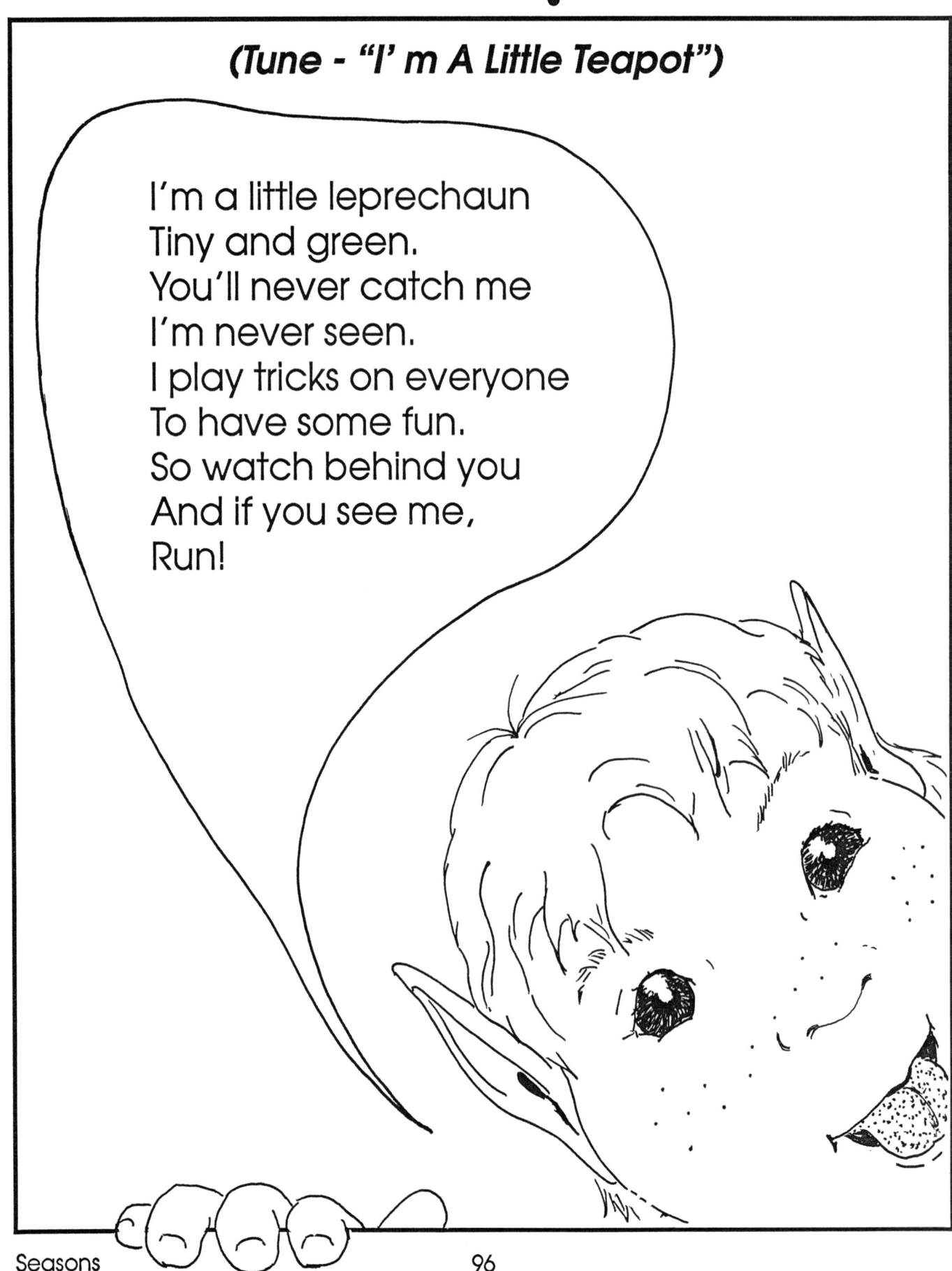

I'm A Little Leprechaun

(Tune - "I'm A Little Teapot")

I'm a little leprechaun
Tiny and green.
You'll never catch me
I'm never seen.
I play tricks on everyone
To have some fun.
So watch behind you
And if you see me,
Run!

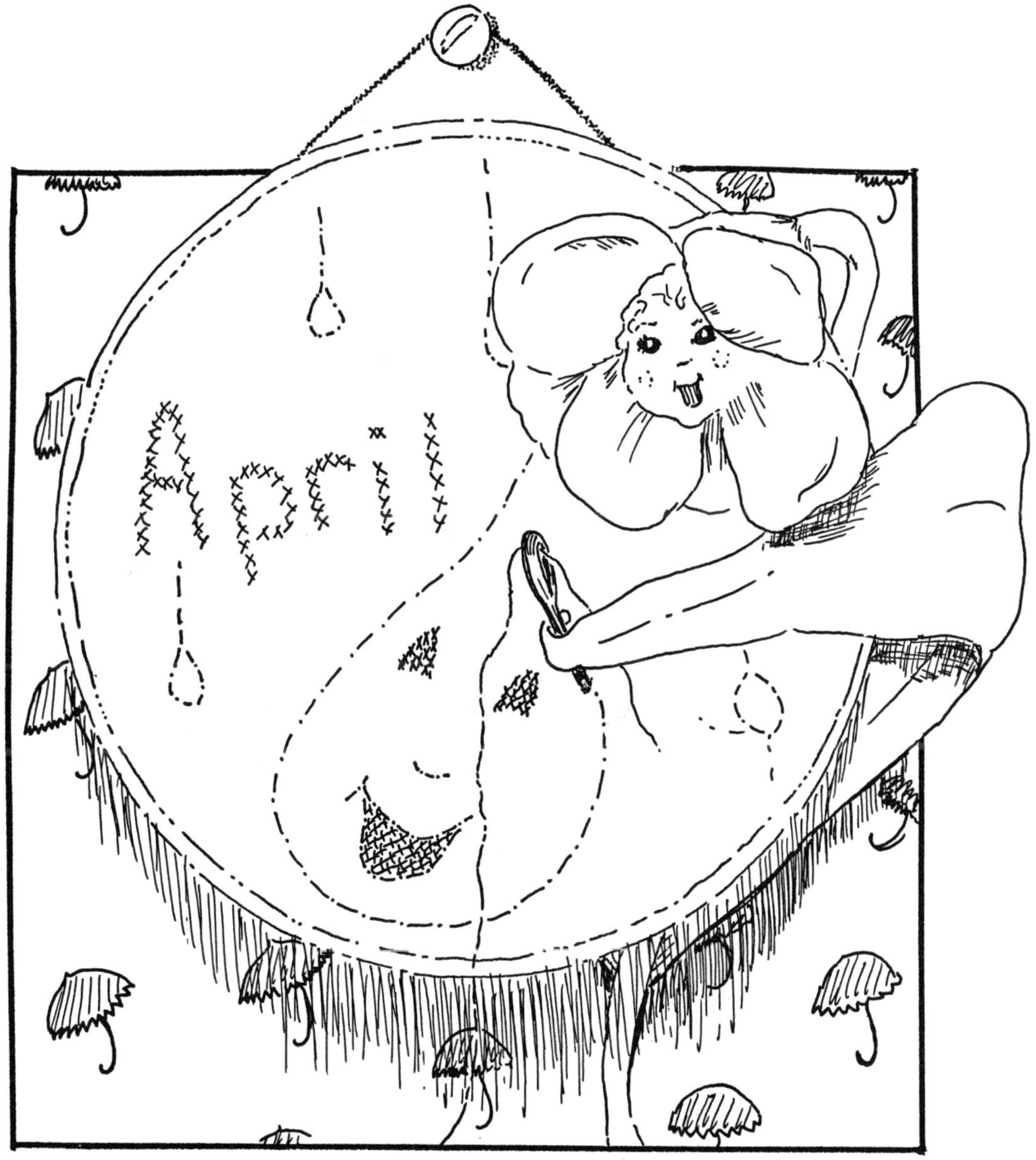
April

Spring In The Playground

(Tune - "Up On The Housetop")

Out on the playground
All around.
You can hear many different sounds.
Watch the swings go way up high,
They can almost reach the sky.

Come let's go,
Don't be slow.
Grab your things,
Away we go.

Bouncing balls and skipping, too,
Spring is here, there's lots to do.

Seasons

Spring Is Here

(Tune - "Jingle Bells")

Spring is here.
Spring is here.
Everything is new.
Look around and hear the sounds,
There's lots of things to do.

Come on out everyone.
Come and play with me.
We can really have some fun,
Cause spring has finally sprung.

Seasons

There are daffodils in bloom.
And flowers everywhere.
Birds are chirping happy tunes;
There's magic in the air.

Spring is here.
Spring is here.
Everything is new.
Look around and hear the sounds,
There's lots of things to do.

Wake Up

Wake up little animals.
Rise today,
Spring is here,
And it's time to play.
Birds are returning and
Building their nests,
Turtles are crawling
Awake from their rest.
Snakes are slithering,
Losing their skin.
The world is ready
For spring to begin.

New Life

Spring brings new life all around,
Budding trees now can be found.
Tulips, daffodils, grass that's green,
Apple trees in bloom are seen.
Baby animals on the farm,
Sounds of new life from the barn.
Piglets, ducklings on the ground,
Spring is new life all around.

Sights of Spring

Ducks and ducklings
In a row.
Watch them waddle
As they go
To the water one-by-one
In they jump to have some fun.

Birds are sitting
In their nests
On the eggs they have to "rest."
Soon you'll hear the familiar sound
Of baby birds chirping all around.

Seasons

Something In The Air

There is something in the air
And it's all around.
Flowers are popping
Their heads up from underneath the ground.
Birds are returning,
And their songs you can hear.
The sun is warmer,
And it seems very near.

Children are skipping in
Playgrounds everywhere.
Kites are flying
Up high in the air.
Signs of spring
In nature abound,
And signs of new life
Can be found.

Birds

(Tune - "Frere Jacques")

Come back robins
Come back robins
Spring is near.
Spring is near.
Everyone is waiting.
Everyone is waiting.
Your songs we want to hear.
Your songs we want to hear.

(These birds can replace robins for variety.)
- bluejays
- sparrows
- seagulls
- geese
- loons
- hummingbirds

Counting In Spring

1 2 3 4 5

Bees are buzzing round their hives.

6 7 8 9 10

Birds from the south are coming back again.

10 9 8 7 6

Time to get our bikes fixed.

5 4 3 2 1

Everyone is out in the sun having fun.

Counting 1 - 10

Animals Returning

(Tune - "Pop Goes The Weasel")

The bears in spring
Come out of their den
And they are really hungry.
They yawn and stretch
And blink at the sun
Cause spring is finally coming.

The turtles in spring
Come out of their shells
And slowly they start moving.
They stretch their necks
And look around
To see that spring is coming.

The squirrels in spring
Come out of their homes
And all around they're running.
They look for food
And scurry about
Cause spring is finally coming.

The bees in spring
Come out of their hives
And all around are buzzing.
We know that honey
They will make
Cause spring is finally coming.

Rain

Pitter patter

Pitter patter

Rain is falling down.

Puddles everywhere

Are covering the ground.

Ducks are marching

In the water one-by-one.

Grab your umbrella

And we'll go have some fun.

Pitter patter

Pitter patter

Rain is falling down.

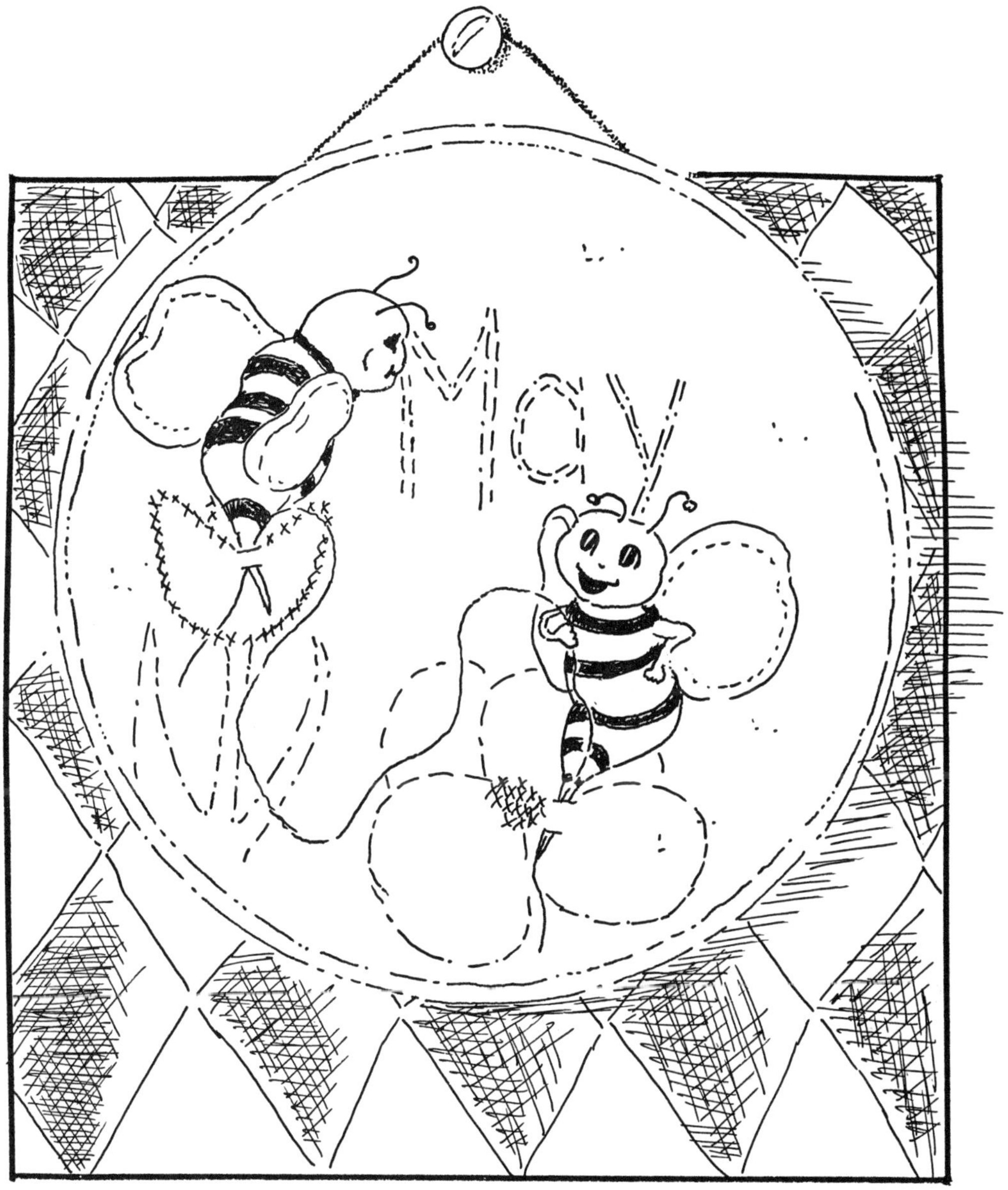
May

May

May is the month

Lovely flowers are in bloom,

And the air is filled with

Scents of their perfume.

The sky is blue

And the sun shines bright,

And at times there's a breeze

To fly my kite.

May is the month

Of colors all around,

Green, yellow, red, and gold

Cover the ground.

Flowers

(Action Poem)

One little flower popped its head up from the ground,

It was all alone, and it slowly looked around.

Then the sun started shining

And a gentle wind blew,

And now in the flower bed

Counting, Addition, Movement

There were two.

Two little flowers just starting to grow

The sun kept shining

And it rained some more,

And soon blooming were flowers three and four.

Time went by, and flower one looked around,

And flowers were everywhere, covering the ground.

Follow The Leader

(Action Verse)

I am Mrs. Duck
And I can see
My little ducklings
Waddling after me.

I am Mrs. Frog
And I can see
My little froggies
Leaping after me.

I am Mrs. Bird
And I can see
My little birdies
Flying after me.

I am Mrs. Rabbit
And I can see
All my bunnies
Bouncing after me.

I am Mrs. Hen
And I can see
All my little chicks
Hopping after me.

Animals And Their Young, Movement

I am Mr. Horse
And I can see
Small little ponies
Galloping after me.

I am Mr. Snake
And my little ones can be found
Slithering low, down on the ground.

I am Mr. Bear
And I can see
My little bear cubs
Stomping after me.

I am Mr. Kangaroo
And I can see
All my babies
Jumping after me.

I am the teacher
And I can see
All my pupils
Running after me.

Sights In May

(Tune - "I'm A Little Teapot" Action Verse)

I'm a little rosebud
Curled up tight
I stay inside, warm at night.
But when the sun shines down on me,
I open up for the world to see.

I'm a little sparrow
I'm flying free.
Up in the blue sky, look at me.
I swoop down so I can eat.
A juicy worm is a special treat.

I'm a giant oak tree
Standing tall.
All around me insects crawl.
I stretch my branches way out wide,
And beneath them you can hide.

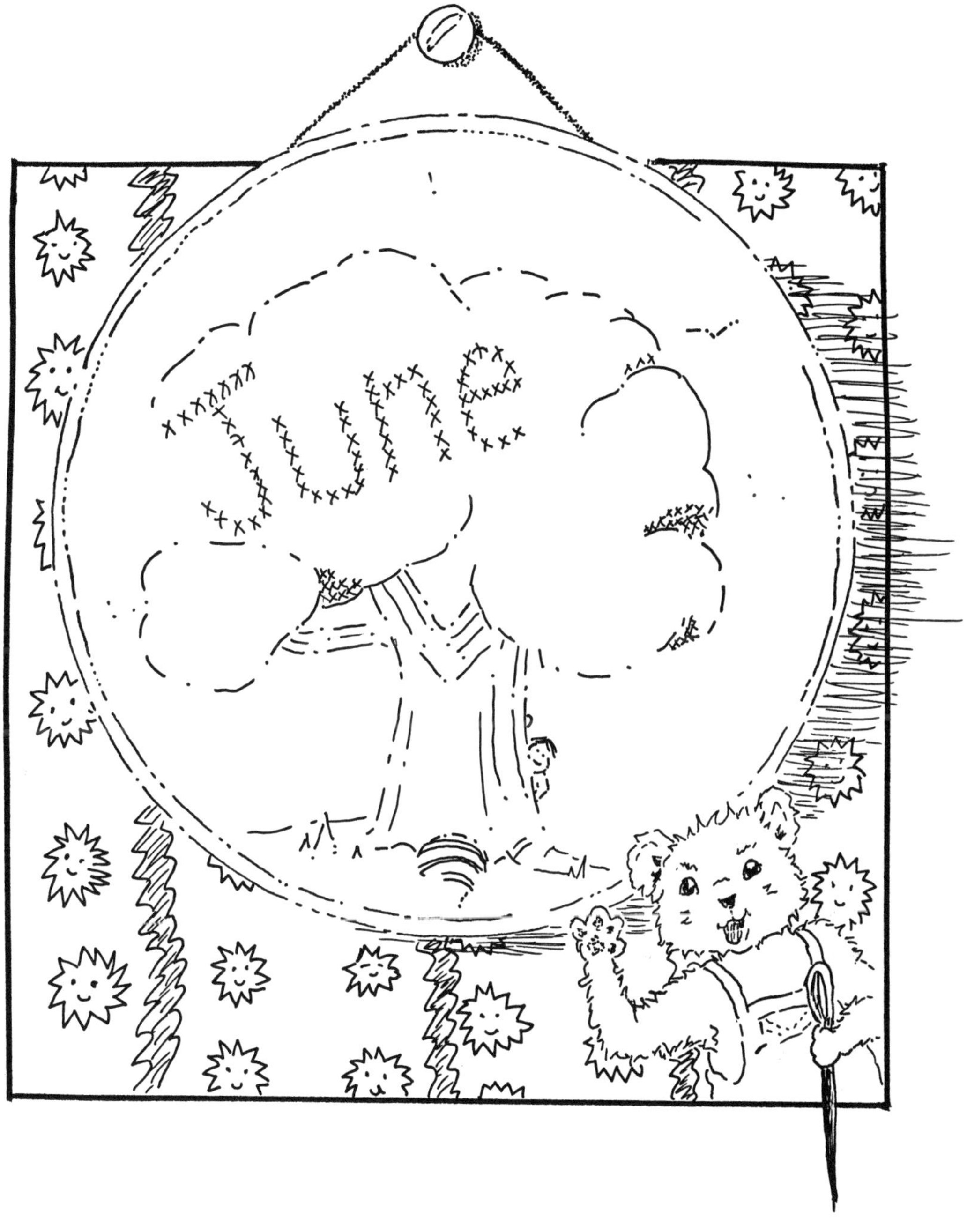
June

June

June is the month
That I like best.
Summer is here
And I can rest.
Soon school will be over
We'll put our books away.
And spend our time
Having fun all day.
The end of school is coming;
I can hardly wait.
I'll watch TV
And stay up late.

Seasons

Little Children

(Tune - "Twinkle Twinkle Little Star")

Little children out to play,
On this sunny, warm June day.
Soon school and work will be done
We'll spend our time having fun.
Little children out to play,
On this sunny, warm June day.

(Tune - "I'm A Little Teapot")

I'm a little boy (girl)
And I'm glad to say.
School will be over,
I'll be on my way.
When the bell rings
I'll count to four,
Cross the room
And go out the door.

Seasons

Field Trip

Five little children on a field trip in June
Gathering flowers and humming a tune.
They decided to stop and sing a song
And wait for the others to come along.

Soon **five** more children came by that day
With rocks they had collected along the way.
Then all the children sat on the ground
And waited for others and looked around.

Not long after **five** more came through
With treasures they found both old and new.
Now they're together with the things they've found.
Can you guess how many are gathered round?

Numbers, Addition

Counting, Playing Games

(Tune - "This Old Man")

Little boy count to **1**
Turn around and have some fun.
Counting, playing games at school,
Following the golden rule.

Little girls count to **2**
Turn around and touch their shoes.
Counting, playing games at school,
Following the golden rule.

Little boys count to **3**
Bend right down and touch your knee.
Counting, playing games at school,
Following the golden rule.

Counting 1 - 10, Self-Awareness

Little girls count to **4**
Jump up high then touch the floor.
Counting, playing games at school,
Following the golden rule.

Little boys count to **5**
Spin around and come alive.
Counting, playing games at school,
Following the golden rule.

All the children count to **10**
Run away, come back again.
Counting, playing games at school,
Following the golden rule.

Be Like...

(Action Rhymes)

Be like frogs
Hopping in the sun,
Jumping up and down
And having fun.

Be like fish
Swimming to and fro,
Moving their fins
Fast and slow.

Be like birds
Flying high and low,
Flapping their wings
Wherever they go.

Be like snakes
Crawling on the ground,
Slipping through the grass
And moving all around.

Positional Concepts

(Action Rhymes)

Be like ponies
Galloping on their way,
Prancing up and down
And having fun today.

Be like mice
Scurrying round a tree,
Moving fast
And staying free.

Be like ducks
Waddling to the lake,
Moving back and forth
Getting through the gate.

Be like the wind
Rushing all around,
Blowing trees
And things on the ground.